MW01228988

A Gift of Mistletoe

Stories, Quotes & Poetry About Holiday Garlands & Greenery

by
John P. Beilenson

design by
Michel Design

PETER PAUPER PRESS, INC.
WHITE PLAINS · NEW YORK

*To David and Jennifer Sawyer,
whose lives, like mistletoe, are symbols of
reconciliation and love*

Copyright © 1991
Peter Pauper Press, Inc.
202 Mamaroneck Avenue
White Plains, New York 10601
ISBN 0-88088-220-4
Printed in Hong Kong
7 6 5 4 3 2 1

Sitting under the mistletoe
(Pale green, fairy mistletoe)
One last candle burning low,
All the sleepy dancers gone,
Just one candle burning on.
Shadows lurking everywhere:
Someone came and kissed me there.

Walter De la Mare

The History of Mistletoe

Magical mistletoe, perhaps the most romantic of all Christmas traditions, has a long and pagan past.

Mistletoe was sacred to the Druids in old Britain, who believed that it possessed endless virtues. Each November, the Arch-Druid, followed by a long procession of priests, would walk into the forest. A tree was chosen, and the Arch-Druid would ascend and cut the hallowed vine. Gathered below, a group of virgins, their skirts spread, would catch the mistletoe before it could touch the ground. This elaborate ritual reinforced the spiritual power of what the Druids called *quidhel* or "all-heal," said to remedy diseases, fight off animals, and fend off witchcraft and other evil spirits.

In Scandinavian mythology, it is said that the wicked spirit Loki used a branch of mistletoe as the dart that killed Balder, "the whitest and most beloved of all the gods." According to the legend, however, Balder's mother Freyja redeemed the plant, honoring the memory of her son. Mistletoe

4

thus became a symbol of joy and peace. From then on, when enemies in Europe's northern forests would meet under mistletoe, they would lay down their arms and keep a truce until the next day.

Mistletoe, viewed by the Church during the Middle Ages as a remnant of Europe's heathen past, was eventually rehabilitated and "Christianized." Just before the Reformation, clergy at England's Cathedral of York began bringing a large bundle of mistletoe into the cathedral each Christmas. This healing plant served as a symbol of Christ, the Divine Healer of all people and nations.

In the years that followed, the people of England introduced mistletoe into their homes, where the more familiar traditions surrounding the plant then developed. Hanging mistletoe in a doorway or from the ceiling became a sign of good will and harmony to all visitors—a throwback to mistletoe's ancient role as a "plant of peace."

In old England, kissing under the mistletoe was considered a sincere pledge of love and marriage. In fact,

without a kiss under the plant at Christmas, one's chances of exchanging vows during the following year were slim.

This traditional ritual began when a man kissed a woman under the mistletoe. He then took a berry off the plant, and saved each berry as a token of the couple's love. When all the berries were plucked, all the kissing was done. On the Twelfth and final night of Christmas, the mistletoe was burned. It was believed that if the mistletoe were not burned, the couples who kissed beneath it would never marry.

Today, mistletoe remains a symbol of warmth and friendship, happiness and good luck. And while a kiss under the mistletoe may not be interpreted as a sincere pledge of love, it still warms the heart and adds a healthy dose of mischief and good cheer to the holidays.

The Magical Mistletoe

At every Christmas celebration:
Fragrant wreaths, candles lit and all
  aglow,
The creamy egg nog offers sweet
  libation,
But don't forget the magic—the
  mistletoe.

Clung to oak, a plant mysterious,
With curled leaf and hardened berry,
It blooms in dark forests delirious
With powers for making peace, for
  making merry.

In the home, it dangles from the ceiling
Among the holly evergreen and red,
It reconciles friends and family, healing
All who pause beneath. And it is said,

If below you steal a kiss, spark a blaze,
Your love will burn for many
  Christmas days.

J. B.

The mistletoe bough at our Christmas
  board
Shall hang, to the honor of Christ the
  Lord:
For He is the evergreen tree of Life. . . .
                                    English Song

The Language of Christmas Flowers

Mistletoe, the symbol of healing and good will, is not the only Christmas plant or flower that carries with it an interesting tradition. Many of the following plants are evergreens and, as such, symbols of the holiday, of life everlasting. Others have more particular stories, relating to the story of the birth or life of Christ. Woven together, these botanical traditions form a literary wreath as enjoyable as the sight and scent of the plants and flowers themselves.

Deck the halls with boughs of holly,
Tra la la la la, la la la la
'Tis the season to be jolly,
Tra la la la la, la la la la.

Considered today by some to be the ultimate Christmas plant, holly was first revered among the early Romans and northern Barbarians, who chewed it for courage, hung it as a charm against evil, and gave it as presents during the winter solstice. One legend held that sprites lived in holly trees, and that draping holly boughs indoors with the advent of winter provided warmth and cheer for these jolly spirits.

With the rise of Christianity, holly was converted to a powerful symbol of Christ's life. The red berries became Christ's blood. The white flowers stood for His purity. The sharp, pointed leaves were His crown of thorns, and the plant's bitter bark His agony on the Cross.

Colonists in America, searching for reminders of Christmas in England, were happy to find the abundant American Holly *(Ilex opaca)* growing in New England and the Ohio Valley. Today, during the holidays, holly is used throughout the home, where it decorates tables, walls and doors.

But give me holly, bold and jolly
Honest, prickly, shining holly;
Pluck me holly leaf and berry
For the day when I make merry.

Christina Rossetti

Ivy

In Roman days, ivy was the signature plant of Bacchus, the wine-god, and symbolized wild drinking and feasting. Later, Christians frowned on this orgiastic reference and banned the vine from inside their homes, allowing ivy to grow only on the outside walls.

Ivy survived its scandalous reputation and became one of England's, and later America's, favorite plants—both indoors and out. In many old Christmas songs, holly is represented as the male plant, while ivy is the female. This lyrical comparison served as a way of debating which sex should rule the household.

Today, ivy is loved not for its controversial past, but simply for its rich color and for its usefulness as an attractive rope for Christmas wreaths.

13

Rosemary

Once one of Christmas' most popular plants, rosemary is now not generally recognized as a holiday green. Legend has it, however, that rosemary was sacred to Mary and developed its delicate scent when she first hung the Baby Jesus' swaddling clothes on it to dry.

While rosemary's bloom is deep lavender, according to Spanish sources it was originally white. The transformation occurred when, during the flight into Egypt, Mary cast her purple robe over a rosemary bush while resting with Joseph and the Baby Jesus.

Today, these traditions are largely forgotten, although small bunches of the fresh herb make an appropriate and sweet-smelling addition to any holiday wreath, decoration or potpourri.

Poinsettias and Christmas Roses

While rosemary has lost its appeal, poinsettias, with their red, pink, or white flowers, have become an increasingly popular addition to Christmas flora.

Native to Central America, the plant is named for Dr. Joel Roberts Poinsett, who served as U. S. Ambassador to Mexico in the 1820's. When he returned, he brought the broad-leafed plant to South Carolina, where it spread widely.

In Mexico, the plant is called "the flower of the Holy Night," and the following Mexican legend explains this appellation:

A young shepherd boy (the story goes) traveled with the Three Wise Men to offer gifts to the Christ Child. Because he did not have a gift for the baby, the boy prayed fervently and contritely while the group paused in their journey. When the boy arose, the poinsettia miraculously grew where he had knelt. His prayers answered, the boy took a stalk of the

plant with its vermilion blooms, entered the manger, and laid his gift at the feet of the Christ Child.

In European versions of this story, the poinsettias were Christmas Roses, and a young shepherd girl followed along without a gift. As she walked along sadly, it is said, an angel appeared and strew white roses in her path, and she took them to the infant Jesus.

Once called "Christ's herb," the Christmas Rose was believed to have strong powers—curing gout, cholera and frightening off evil spirits.

Today, the Christmas Rose is still loved because it blooms twice, once in the spring, and again in the middle of winter—sometimes on the very Day of Epiphany.

*At Christmas I no more desire a rose
Than wish a snow in May's new-fangled
    mirth;
But like of each thing that in season
    grows.*

William Shakespeare

Hawthorn

Most hawthorns are not considered Christmas plants, but the Glastonbury (Haw)thorn has a special place in Christmas mythology.

English lore claims that the plant stems from the staff of the missionary Joseph of Arimathea. The thorn, it is said, took root the first time Joseph placed his walking stick in the soil of the British Isles. The plant blossoms twice a year—in the spring and, like the Christmas Rose, around the Day of Epiphany.

Laurel

The laurel is an ancient Roman symbol of triumph, glory and joy. Early Christians used laurel wreaths as Christmas decorations to celebrate the victory over death that Christ's coming signifies. A German carol, in the words of the Three Wise Men, relates:

> *From afar we come, and our staves*
> *Are adorned with laurel;*
> *To seek Jesus, the King,*
> *   the Saviour great.*
> *And to bring Him laurel.*

Laurel wreaths, also a Roman tradition of celebration and victory, are today hung on doors as a friendly seasonal greeting.

Lady's Bedstraw

Reputed to cure snakebite and earache, Lady's Bedstraw, a delicate grassy plant, was thought to be part of the manger hay on which Christ was born. After the Child's birth, it is related, the Lady's Bedstraw burst into bloom. This plant, also called yellow bedstraw, has a squarish stem, grows close to the ground, and produces tiny yellow flowers that look like a little cloud or mist.

The Cherry Tree

The cherry tree has a special place in Christmas celebrations in Central Europe. There, people break off branches of this tree at the beginning of Advent and place them indoors in pots of water. The warm air causes the twigs to bloom and, by Christmas, cherry blossoms fill the house. The blossoms are considered good luck charms. According to legend, a young woman who tends a twig carefully will find a husband in the next year if the bloom is produced on Christmas Eve.

Today, cherry blossoms, like other flowering plants, are little miracles in and of themselves. Like the miraculous birth of Christ, they remind us that even in darkest, coldest winter, spring's warmth and light are never far behind.

In one version of *The Cherry Tree Carol*, a beloved Christmas poem and song, Mary asks Joseph to pluck a cherry off a tree for her. Joseph answers: *Let him pluck thee a cherry who is father to thy child*. At that point the Babe within Mary's womb instructs:

> *Go to the tree, Mary,*
> *And it shall bow to thee,*
> *And the highest branch of all*
> *Shall bow down to Mary's knee.*

Joseph then realizes that Mary's baby is the Christ Child.

O Christmas Tree,
O Christmas Tree

O Christmas tree, O Christmas tree,
Thy leaves are green forever.
O Christmas tree, O Christmas tree,
Thy beauty leaves thee never.

Thy leaves are green in summer's prime,
Thy leaves are green at Christmas time.
O Christmas tree, O Christmas tree,
Thy leaves are green forever.

German Christmas Carol

The long tradition of many plants notwith-
standing, Christmas trees are the floral focal
point of modern Christmas.

Trees, like the plants previously described, have long been worshipped from Egypt to India as symbols of regeneration and life. The development of the Christmas tree, however, probably stems from a 10th Century legend that describes how on the night Christ was born, all the trees, although covered in ice and snow, flowered and bore fruit.

A later German folk tale tells the story of a shivering child who came to a woodcutter's home in the middle of winter. The child was warmly welcomed and given a bed in which to sleep. That morning, a choir of angels sang in the sky, and the woodcutter and his family discovered that they had cared for the Christ Child the night before. The Child then plucked a twig from a fir tree, and planted it. And upon leaving, he vowed that the tree would never fail to bear fruit at Christmas and that the woodcutter's family would always live in abundance.

25

The origin of the domestic Christmas tree is often ascribed to Martin Luther. One Christmas in the middle of the 16th Century, it is said, the Great Reformer took a walk outside and was entranced by the stars and nature's beauty. When he came home, he told his children to set up a tree and attach candles to symbolize the beautiful heavens that had produced Jesus.

In the ensuing centuries, the German Christmas tree grew more elaborate. Candy canes, glass balls, cookies, sweets, and oranges were used to decorate the tree, and a star was generally placed on the top—traditions that remain in one form or another to this day.

While 18th Century German immigrants to the United States brought many of their customs with them, Christmas was officially suppressed in some parts of the colonies, particularly New England.

Indeed, we must travel back to England and wait until the middle of the 19th Century and

the reign of Queen Victoria and Prince Albert (who was of German stock) to trace the origin of the Christmas tree's popularity, both in Britain and America.

In 1841, Victoria and Albert for the first time placed fir trees in the center of Christmas celebrations. The couple decorated a table-top tree to the delight of children and adults. The custom quickly spread, and these trees grew in size until they had to be taken off the table. Soon the Christmas tree became the symbol of a family-oriented Christmas—on both sides of the Atlantic.

Victorian decorations were edible—shiny red apples, strings of popcorn, walnuts painted gold, barley sugar, and other confections. In fact, early trees were often called "sugartrees," owing to the sweet quality of the decorations. When the tree was dismantled on January 5th, the Eve of Epiphany, the sweets would be raffled off to a family's eager children.

The English passion for Christmas trees soon found its way back across the Atlantic, where, with the help of a second wave of German immigrants, the tree became firmly ensconced in American Christmas. Today, electric lights, wooden toys, and beautiful ornaments grace contemporary Christmas trees.

Tinsel, another popular decoration, might seem like a recent addition to the Christmas tree, but in fact its origins date back to the following legend: A good woman with a large family trimmed her tree elaborately. On the night of Christmas Eve, spiders came upon the beautifully decorated tree and wove webs all around it. The Christ Child, however, to reward the woman for her goodness, blessed the tree, and the webs turned to glittering silver.

While Christmas today is generally less miraculous than the legend of tinsel, stories like this one express some of the magic that is rekindled each Christmas season, when families come together, and people open their hearts to one another.

Bring forth the fir tree,
The box and the bay,
Deck out our cottage
For glad Christmas Day.
Anonymous

Advent
Wreaths

In many churches, the four Sundays before
Christmas are observed as Advent Sundays.
Advent wreaths, as well as Advent calendars
and candelabras, remind people of the season
and help prepare them for the holiday. For this
reason, an Advent wreath should be hung
where everyone can see it. Each Advent
Sunday a candle is added to the wreath, and on
Christmas itself an even larger candle is lit in
the center.

Christmas Potpourri

Little evokes the memory of Christmas past more than the swirling scents of trees and wreaths, a crackling Yule fire, fresh-baked Christmas cookies and cakes, popping corn for the tree, and, of course, the crisp smell of the cold December air dancing off visitors as they come into your home.

Our favorite bowl of Christmas potpourri is guaranteed to recreate this holiday atmosphere. It's a redolent mixture that's sure to please the senses, silence any lingering humbugs, and bring back the spirit of a traditional Christmas—at any time of the year.

1 quart fragrant pine needles
1 dozen small pine cones
1 cup bay leaves
1 cup bayberry leaves
3 cups sassafras leaves
3 cups orange peel
1 cup cinnamon sticks
1/2 cup whole cloves

Make this recipe by the (dry) gallon, as its popularity causes its disappearance by the basketful. A lot of pleasure comes with the gathering of needles and cones. Brown needles or fresh green ones can be used. If the needles are very long, they can be cut, by the handful, to about two inches in length. Cones, if larger than a teacup, may be incorporated after other ingredients are mixed.

Bay leaves and bayberry leaves can be left whole. Use oak, magnolia, orange or holly in place of, or in addition to, the sassafras leaves. Tree leaves are used fresh or dry, with about one half of them crushed or broken at the time of mixing.

Save, and dry, orange and other citrus peels throughout the year for the potpourri. Cinnamon sticks broken to three-inch lengths or less, and whole cloves, complete the recipe. Happy aromatic holidays!

*Everywhere, everywhere, Christmas
   tonight!
Christmas in lands of the fir-tree and
   pine,
Christmas in lands of the palm-tree and
   vine . . .
Everywhere, everywhere, Christmas
   tonight!*

Phillips Brooks

MW01229552

UNLOCKING THE
INTROVERT

A POCKET GUIDE TO UNDERSTANDING
AND INTERACTING WITH INTROVERTS

ANTONIA O. ALLEN

Society of Introverts Publishing LLC
New York

All rights are reserved under the information and Pan-American copyright conventions.

First published in the United States of America.

All rights reserved. No part of this book may be reproduced, distributed, or transmitted in any form or by any means, including photocopying, recording, or other electronic or mechanical methods, without the prior written permission of the publisher, except in the case of brief quotations embodied in critical reviews and certain other noncommercial uses permitted by copyright law.

DISCLAIMER

The information provided in this book is for informational purposes only. The author and publisher make no representations or warranties concerning the accuracy or completeness of the contents of this book and specifically disclaim any implied warranties of merchantability or fitness for a particular purpose. The advice and strategies contained herein may not be suitable for every situation. Readers should consult with a professional where appropriate.

Permissions: For permissions to reproduce or distribute any part of this book, please contact Society of Introverts Publishing LLC at www.socicietyofintroverts.com.

Published by: Society of Introverts Publishing LLC

Printed in the United States of America

Copyright © 2024 by Antonia O. Allen

ISBN: ISBN: 979-8-9907238-0-1

DEDICATION

To my fellow introverts, your quiet power and deep introspection reflections light up the world in profound and life-changing ways. My dear introverts, you are the unsung heroes of resilience, sensitivity, and creativity. I dedicate this book to each of you with the most profound respect and appreciation for your contributions to our shared path of self-awareness and camaraderie. These pages will be a source of knowledge and encouragement for you, leading you toward a more empowered, accepting, and self-loving you.

TABLE OF CONTENTS

ACKNOWLEDGEMENTS

My mother, for being all that then some, always supporting me, and for never making me feel like her "weird" child.

Andrew (@tgdesigns45) for being patient and the greatest in the creative world.

My mentors: Ash Cash, Storm Leroy, Marvin Mitchell, and my Path to Prosperity (P2P) family.

My Coach, Dr. Martin Pratt. I am grateful that God sent you, my way.

INTRODUCTION

Acknowledging and valuing introverts' distinctive traits and requirements in a society that frequently values extroversion is essential. Welcome to "Unlocking the Introvert: A Pocket Guide to Understanding and Interacting with Introverts."

This book serves as a guide for understanding the complex inner lives of introverts, developing deep connections, and building welcoming surroundings that support their success.

Why would some people rather be alone than attend social events? Or why do some people seem more comfortable in one-on-one situations yet may find big crowds intimidating?

Understanding introversion is about accepting the wide range of human personalities

and communication styles, not just labels. In the upcoming chapters, we will explore the nuances of loving, interacting with, and working with introverts.

This book provides valuable advice for introverts and people who engage with them, covering everything from organizing activities that suit their interests to effective dispute-resolution techniques.

As you set out on this adventure, think about the following queries:

- What false beliefs about introverts do you have, and how might they affect how you interact with them?
- How can you design spaces that respect introverts' need for privacy and introspection without making them feel alone?
- How might an awareness of introversion improve your connections both at work and in your personal life?

Come along with me as we explore the wonders of introversion and celebrate the diversity of viewpoints. Are you prepared to develop stronger relationships and help introverts reach their full potential? Now, let's get started.

CHAPTER 1

LOVING AN INTROVERT

"I wish I could show you when you are lonely or in darkness the astonishing light of your being." – Hafiz of Shiraz

- Introversion is a normal part of personality.
- Appreciate the introvert's quiet power.
- Communication is essential in any relationship.

It takes more than devotion to love an introvert. You also need to recognize and value introvert's characteristics and preferences. Environments that facilitate solitude and contemplation are frequently conducive to introverts' well-being. In this chapter, we'll look at ways to have a happy and encouraging connection with the introverts in your life.

Above all, it's critical to understand that introversion is a normal part of personality, not a defect that somebody must correct. Appreciate the introvert's quiet power and recognize the depth of the introvert's feelings and ideas rather than attempting to change them. Put yourself in their position and acknowledge their desire for privacy to develop empathy.

To illustrate*: John and Emily have been married for several years. John is outgoing and enjoys social situations, and Emily is a reserved introvert who cherishes her privacy. John initially found it challenging to*

comprehend Emily's need for so much alone time, and he frequently felt betrayed when she chose to spend time alone rather than participate in activities with him. However, after frank and open discussions, John learned to respect Emily's desire for privacy and realized that it didn't mean she didn't feel the same way for him. He discovered the best way to help her was to allow her the autonomy to unwind independently, whether reading quietly in the evenings or going for long walks outdoors. John and Emily developed a loving relationship that respected their introverted and extroverted traits by showing empathy and understanding for one another.

Communication is essential in any relationship, but it becomes much more so when one is in love with an introvert. Please give them room to express themselves and do it at their leisure. Introverts frequently prefer in-depth, meaningful talks to casual banter, so they listen intently

and actively without passing judgment or interjecting.

Offer chances for interactions that suit their comfort zone and areas of interest. Make time for meaningful moments with your partner, whether a peaceful trek in the woods or a comfortable evening reading a good book. Remember to show respect and support by acknowledging and celebrating their achievements and milestones.

Lastly, remember that there are many ways to show someone you love them. Introverts can show affection by being friendly, considerate, or present. You should love the richness and depth that an introvert adds to your life and accept the beauty of being in a relationship with one.

Questions for contemplation:

- *How do you now show introverted people that you love and care about them?*
- *What changes can you consider better to respect their desire for quiet time and introspection?*
- *How can you improve your relationship with them by learning more about their preferences and personality traits?*

CHAPTER 2

BEING FRIENDS WITH AN INTROVERT

"Beware of those who seek constant crowds; they are nothing alone." – Charles Bukowski

- Be considerate of their social preferences and boundaries.
- Engage in genuine empathy and active listening.
- Acknowledge and honor their successes and show you care about them.

Establishing and preserving connections with introverts requires time, tolerance, under-standing, and a readiness to adjust to their communication and social preferences. This chapter will cover methods for developing deep connections with introverts and setting up surroundings conducive to their success.

First, it's critical to understand that introverts typically have narrower social circles and value close, personal relationships above fleeting exchanges. Value the quality of your contacts and the depth of your conversations rather than anticipating massive group gatherings or continuous communication.

To illustrate: Though Toni is gregarious and outgoing, Ekanem is a contemplative introvert who enjoys smaller, more private parties. The two have been friends since college. Toni initially had a hard time understanding Eka-nem's need for peace; she would frequently mistake it for aloofness or indifference.

However, Toni tried to accept and value Ekanem's reserved personality as their friendship developed. Instead of going on big group outings, she learned to start one-on-one hangouts, giving Ekanem the cozy setting he liked. When Ekanem felt appreciated and understood, he became more open and honest with Toni about his feelings. As they accepted one another's differences and looked out for one another's needs, their friendship grew and solidified into a long-lasting relationship based on respect and understanding.

Be considerate of their social preferences and boundaries. Recognize that introverts can require some alone time to recover from social activities, and don't be offended if they turn down invitations or choose more intimate get-togethers. Being tolerant and flexible is crucial when developing a friendship with an introvert. Make time for one-on-one get-togethers or activities that suit their interests. Introverts frequently flourish in calmer, more

laid-back environments where they may have meaningful talks without being overstimulated by outside stimuli. Ask them to watch movies at home, go on coffee dates, or take nature walks.

When interacting with your introverted pals, engage in genuine empathy and active listening. Acknowledge their feelings and opinions and express gratitude for their distinct viewpoints and insights. Be kind and patient, allowing them to express themselves freely and without feeling compelled.

Lastly, acknowledge and honor their successes and show them you care about them. Encourage and reassure them when they encounter difficulties, and be present to enjoy each accomplishment, no matter how tiny. The benefits of friendship with an introvert are immense, but it takes a journey of mutual acceptance and understanding.

Questions for contemplation:

- *With the introverts in your life, how can you create opportunities for meaningful one-on-one interactions?*
- *How can you show them you respect and understand their need for time to unwind and refuel?*
- *How can you be an encouraging and supporting friend to introverts in happy and challenging times?*

CHAPTER 3

COMMUNICATING WITH AN INTROVERT

"Sometimes quiet people really do have a lot to say... they're just being careful about who they open up to."
– *Susan Gale*

- Active listening is crucial when speaking with introverts.
- Use written communication techniques like email or texting.

- Actively hear what they say without getting defensive.

Any connection must be on effective communication, and engaging with introverts requires a grasp of their communication preferences. This chapter will cover methods for encouraging meaningful and transparent communication with introverts, so everyone feels heard and understood.

Respecting introverts' need for deliberate contemplation before answering is crucial to effective communication. Before voicing their opinions, introverts frequently need time to absorb information internally. Give them time to consider their answers without hurrying or interfering.

Active listening is crucial when speaking with introverts. Maintain eye contact, nod in agreement, and give vocal and nonverbal indications that you comprehend their words. Since introverts may find asserting themselves in

social situations difficult, avoid taking over the conversation or interjecting.

To encourage conversation with introverts, use written communication techniques like email or texting. They can express themselves more freely and deliberately in written communication because they do not feel constrained by the need to read social cues or provide an instant answer.

To illustrate: Sarah struggles to speak up at work team meetings because she is an introvert. Taking note of her reserved demeanor, her manager begins forwarding agendas ahead of time and invites team members to provide feedback via email before the meeting. This method allows Sarah to contribute her views with more ease and assurance.

Approach conversations with delicate subjects or resolve disputes with introverts with understanding and tact. Select a calm, private space where people can express themselves

honestly. Employ "I" words to voice your emotions and worries without blaming others, and actively hear what they say without getting defensive. Modifying your communication style to suit introverts' needs may cultivate stronger bonds and make the atmosphere more welcoming and encouraging for everyone.

Questions for contemplation:

- *How can you facilitate an environment where introverts feel free to express themselves during conversations?*
- *What techniques can you use to show that you are genuinely interested in what they are saying and that you are actively listening to them?*
- *How can you modify your communication style in both social and professional contexts to encourage conversation and understanding with introverts?*

CHAPTER 4

SUPPORTING AN INTROVERT

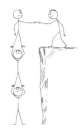

"I talked to a calzone for fifteen minutes last night before I realized it was just an introverted pizza. I wish all my acquaintances were so tasty." – Jarod Kintz

- Give introverts the time and space they need to unwind and refuel.
- Establish a secure and encouraging environment.

- Give introverts chances to grow and develop.

It's essential to recognize the unique requirements of introverts and provide them with the support and encouragement they need to flourish. In this chapter, we'll look at how to give introverts significant support, covering anything from career aspirations to personal obstacles.

Respecting introverts' need for time to reflect is one of the most crucial strategies for helping them. Give introverts the time and space they need to unwind and refuel without interruption or pressure, as they frequently find inspiration and energy in quiet periods of meditation.

Providing introverts with emotional support entails acknowledging their emotions and giving an unbiased listening ear. Establish a secure and encouraging environment where people may freely share their ideas and

feelings because they know that those feelings are acknowledged and appreciated.

Give introverts chances to grow and develop so they can follow their interests and passions. Motivate and inspire them as they work toward their objectives. Say something positive and encouraging about their success, no matter how small.

To illustrate: David, an introvert, has always wanted to launch his own company but is afraid to take the risk. Seeing his potential, his mentor provides direction and encouragement, working with him to create a business plan and assisting at every step. With the help of his mentor, David feels more confident about going after his entrepreneurial goals.

By being aware of introverts' unique requirements and providing genuine support, you can promote their personal and professional development and make the workplace more caring and welcoming for everyone.

Questions for contemplation:

- *How can you foster an atmosphere that respects introverts' need for privacy and introspection?*
- *What techniques can you use to provide introverts in your life with emotional support and validation?*
- *How can you empower and inspire introverts to follow their dreams and ambitions with courage and tenacity?*

CHAPTER 5

WORKING WITH AN INTROVERT

"The more powerful and original a mind, the more it will incline towards the religion of solitude." – Aldous Huxley

- Give them a chance to demonstrate their knowledge and inventiveness.
- Establish a cooperative workplace that celebrates differences in viewpoints.
- Give introverts the chance to work in sessions free from interruptions.

In the workplace, it's essential to recognize introverts' preferred working methods and establish a conducive atmosphere for their productive contributions. This chapter will examine ways to work with introverts harmoniously and productively.

Acknowledge and take advantage of introverts' strong points, such as their capacity for critical thought and intense task focus. Give them tasks that let them work on their initiative and give them a chance to demonstrate their knowledge and inventiveness.

To illustrate, Team leader Lisa assigns Tom, an introverted team member with a reputation for analytical prowess, a research project. She trusts him to work independently and offers assistance when needed rather than micromanaging his work. Tom exceeds expectations by providing a thoughtful report that highlights his advantages as an introverted contributor.

Establish a cooperative workplace that celebrates differences in viewpoints and promotes candid communication. Encourage an inclusive and respectful environment where introverts freely express their thoughts and worries without worrying about criticism or rejection.

Acknowledge the significance of striking a balance between individual and teamwork. Give introverts the chance to work in concentrated sessions free from interruptions and team building and collaboration activities.

By being aware of and understanding introverts' working preferences, you can create a more welcoming and practical work atmosphere for all team members.

Questions for contemplation:

- *How can you take advantage of introverts' natural tendencies to improve teamwork and output at work?*

- *What tactics can you use to establish an office culture that encourages candid conversation and recognizes the contributions of introverts?*
- *How can you meet introverts' demand for concentrated concentration by balancing group projects and solitary work time?*

CHAPTER 6

ENCOURAGING AN INTROVERT TO OPEN UP

"I'm very picky with whom I give my energy to. I prefer to reserve my time, intensity and spirit exclusively to those who reflect sincerity." – Dau Voir

- Provide them opportunities to share at their own pace.

- Exercise genuine curiosity and active listening.
- Establish rapport and trust over time.

It takes time, sensitivity, and knowledge of introverts' distinct communication styles to get them to open up. In this chapter, we'll examine methods for fostering an atmosphere that encourages introverts to be authentically themselves.

Recognize and appreciate introverts' need for alone time to gather their ideas and emotions before expressing them to others. Provide them opportunities to share at their own pace rather than pressuring them to open up or reveal information before they're ready.

When conversing with introverts, exercise genuine curiosity and active listening. Ask open-ended questions and express interest in their feelings and views by validating their experiences. Make an accepting environment

where introverts can feel heard and understood.

Establish rapport and trust over time by being dependable, consistent, and considerate of their personal space with introverts. As they progressively get

more at ease discussing their thoughts and feelings with you, be patient and compassionate, and don't breach their confidence by disclosing private information without their permission.

To illustrate: John, who is introverted, progressively shares with his therapist his experiences with sadness and anxiety. John talked about his experiences in a judgment-free environment with the therapist throughout multiple sessions. As their bond grows, John becomes more at ease talking about his feelings and asking for help.

To strengthen your relationships and build deeper connections, you encourage introverts to open up and share their thoughts and feelings more freely by cultivating an environment of patience, empathy, and trust.

Questions for contemplation:

- *How do you make an environment secure and encouraging so introverts may be themselves?*
- *How can you engage with introverts in a way that demonstrates genuine curiosity and active listening so that they are understood and appreciated?*
- *How can you show that you are dependable and considerate of their personal space to gain their trust and eventually get them to open up?*

PLANNING EVENTS FOR AN INTROVERT

"An introversion party is three people sprawled on couches and pillows, reading and occasionally talking."
– Laurie Helgoe

- Consider smaller gatherings rather than big ones.

- Allow them to be alone or in unique, quiet spaces.
- Create inclusive, enjoyable events.

Planning activities accommodating introverts' comfort levels and preferences requires careful effort and knowledge of their demands. This chapter will examine ways to make gatherings welcoming and pleasurable so introverts can fully engage with them.

Consider the event's size and mood; you want to go for more intimate, smaller gatherings rather than big, overpowering crowds. Introverted people tend to do best in environments where they can have long, meaningful talks and establish deeper connections with people.

Give introverts the chance to engage in talks or organized activities at their speed. Consider including group activities or icebreakers that promote conversation without overwhelming shy guests.

To show respect for introverts' need for downtime and relaxation, allow them to be alone or in unique, quiet spaces during events. Permit them to withdraw from the crowd and rest when needed to guarantee that guests may enjoy the event to the fullest without feeling overstimulated.

To illustrate: during a conference, the organizers provide a "quiet room" where participants can unwind and refresh briefly. More introverted attendees value the chance to escape the hectic conference environment and return feeling revitalized.

By considering the needs of introverts when planning events, you can create inclusive, enjoyable events whereby all attendees feel valued and at ease.

Questions for contemplation:

- *How can event size and atmosphere be adjusted to suit the needs of more reserved attendees?*
- *What kind of dialogues or organized activities can you use to promote engagement and communication among introverts?*
- *How can you ensure introverts' comfort and happiness by allowing them to rest and recharge during events?*

CHAPTER 8

TRAVELING WITH AN INTROVERT

"I guess I'm too selfish to travel well with other people," I told Anne later."
— *Alice Steinbach*

- Show respect for introverts' need for leisure and alone time.
- Talk about expectations, interests, and boundaries.
- Accommodate introverts' comfort levels and tastes.

When traveling with them, it's essential to be mindful of introverts' need for privacy, introspection, and meticulous planning. This chapter will look at ways to make travel experiences rewarding and pleasurable while considering introverts' comfort levels.

Include opportunities for rest and solitude in the itinerary to show respect for introverts' need for leisure and alone time when traveling. Make time between activities for introverts to rest and rejuvenate, whether by strolling through a peaceful park, curling up with a book in a quaint cafe, or just spending a moment alone in their hotel room.

Arrange activities that suit the interests and inclinations of introverts, emphasizing quality over quantity. Choose activities that allow for significant experiences and reflection opportunities, such as visiting museums, hiking nature trails, or attending cultural performances,

instead of jam-packing the calendar with back-to-back tours and excursions.

To illustrate: Mike, a shy guy who loves to take pictures, decides to visit a secluded region renowned for its breathtaking scenery. Rather than going on group tours, he walks through the community with his camera, taking personal photos of scenes that speak to him about beauty and peace.

Consider your traveling companions. Be open and cooperative when communicating with introverts to ensure requirements and preferences are met.

Talk about expectations, interests, and boundaries in advance to prevent misunderstandings and disputes during the vacation. It would help if you also understood and tolerated one another's needs.

Adding possibilities for peacefulness, meaningful interactions, and open communication can

make traveling more memorable and enriching. These options will also accommodate introverts' comfort levels and tastes.

Questions for contemplation:

- *What are some ways to accommodate your introverted traveling partners by including opportunities for rest and seclusion in your itinerary?*
- *What activities suit introverts' interests and inclinations, providing opportunities for contemplation and meaningful experiences?*
- *How can you ensure everyone involved has a great and happy travel experience by communicating honestly and cooperatively with introverted travel companions?*

CHAPTER 9

TEACHING AN INTROVERT

"Educating the mind without educating the heart is no education at all." – Aristotle

- Value the learning characteristics of introverts.
- Establish a welcoming and inclusive classroom learning atmosphere.
- Give shy pupils the chance to participate.

When teaching introverts, it's essential to recognize their learning preferences and establish a supportive environment for their academic and psychological success. This chapter will discuss methods for working with introverted students in various learning environments.

Acknowledge and value the learning characteristics of introverts, including their capacity for intense concentration, critical thought, and successful independent study. Give introverted students a chance to learn independently and support them in pursuing subjects aligned with their interests and passions.

Establish a welcoming and inclusive classroom learning atmosphere so shy kids feel appreciated and valued. Encourage an environment of cooperation and respect between all children so that their opinions are acknowledged, and their contributions to society are valued.

Give shy pupils the chance to participate in thought-provoking conversations and freely

voice their opinions in a relaxed setting. Use written assignments, small group activities, and discussion starters to invite shy students to contribute their ideas and viewpoints.

To illustrate: Lynne, a middle school teacher, gives her students writing exercises to promote reflection and self-expression. Tom and other introverted students find it easier to communicate their ideas and emotions in writing, which helps them develop more profound understanding and relationships in the classroom.

By being aware of and adapting their preferred learning methods, you may establish a nurturing and empowering learning environment for introverted students that supports their academic and personal development.

Questions for contemplation:

- *How can you use the learning strengths of introverted students to improve their academic experience?*
- *What techniques can you use to establish a welcoming, inclusive classroom where shy kids feel appreciated and respected?*
- *How can you give introverted pupils the chance to participate in thought-provoking conversations and freely voice their opinions in a relaxed setting?*

CHAPTER 10

CELEBRATING AN INTROVERT

"Introverts listen more than they talk, think before they speak, and often feel as if they express themselves better in writing than in conversation." – Adam S. McHugh

- Give introverts genuine, individualized recognition.
- Allow introverts to express themselves in ways that suit their tastes and interests.

- Consider introverts' boundaries and preferences.

It is essential to acknowledge and value introverts' unique traits and talents while considering their comfort zone and preferences. This chapter will examine ways to design inclusive, meaningful celebrations that appeal to introverts.

Give introverts genuine, individualized recognition for their accomplishments and life milestones. Instead of throwing big, expensive parties, consider more personal and meaningful methods of celebrating, such as a private dinner with close friends or a sincere handwritten note expressing gratitude.

Allow introverts to express themselves in ways that suit their tastes and interests. Provide various celebration options, from low-key events like movie evenings or get-togethers for board games to more daring excursions like hiking or a cultural event.

To illustrate: Mark, an outdoorsy intro-vert, plans a hiking trip with a select group of friends to commemorate his birthday. Together, they create priceless memories that speak to Mark's introverted nature as they spend the day strolling along picturesque trails, taking in the company of one another, and getting in touch with the natural world.

When organizing celebrations, consider intro-verts' boundaries and preferences and avoid surprising or overindulging them. Be transparent and cooperative to ensure the occasion matches their preferences and comfort level.

By planning meaningful, inclusive events that respect introverts' comfort and preferences, you can ensure they are acknowledged and valued for who they are.

Questions for contemplation:

- *How may introverts' milestones and accomplishments be meaningfully honored through personalized celebrations?*
- *What kinds of events and activities suit the interests and celebratory styles of introverts?*
- *How can you honor introverts' limits and preferences when organizing festivities while making them feel valued and at ease?*

CHAPTER 11

MOTIVATING AN INTROVERT

"The greatest gift of life is the ability to be comfortable with yourself, to be who you are, and not feel like you have to live up to anyone else's expectations." – J.R. Rim

- Encourage them to pursue goals that align with their values.
- Give introverts the freedom and authority to pursue their objectives.

- Acknowledge their victories
  and progress.

Understanding introverts' distinct motivations and offering encouragement and assistance suited to their requirements is critical to motivating them. This chapter will cover techniques for inspiring introverts to achieve various life objectives, including career and personal ambitions.

Acknowledge and value introverts' innate drive and enthusiasm for their passions and hobbies. To help introverts feel purposeful and fulfilled, encourage them to pursue goals that align with their values and aspirations rather than depending only on external rewards or recognition.

Give introverts the freedom and authority to pursue their objectives on their terms. Please provide them with direction and assistance, when necessary, but also give them the latitude to take charge of their initiatives and

choices, giving them the flexibility to experiment and explore in their unique ways.

To illustrate: Introverted businessman David starts a tiny internet handcraft company. David keeps authority over the creative process and business operations even as he solicits feedback and counsel from peers and mentors. The solicitation allows him to use his work to communicate his vision and ideals.

Encourage introverts to create attainable goals by segmenting them into minor, more doable activities, and benchmarks. As you support and encourage them, acknowledge their victories and progress along the road to help them stay motivated and focused.

You may effectively inspire introverts to work towards their goals and dreams with passion and commitment by acknowledging their intrinsic motivation, giving them the opportunity for freedom and autonomy, and rewarding their accomplishments.

Questions for contemplation:

- *How can you encourage introverts to pursue their goals by appealing to their innate desire and passion?*
- *What tactics may you use to provide introverts chances to be independent and self-sufficient in their endeavors?*
- *How can you acknowledge and encourage introverts to keep going for their goals by celebrating their small steps forward and successes?*

CHAPTER 12

NEGOTIATING WITH AN INTROVERT

"Empathy is an introvert's superpower." – Jennifer Kahnweiler

- Promote candid communication and teamwork.
- Show empathy and compassion for introverts' needs and priorities.
- Having alternatives will help build a sense of cooperation.

Negotiating with introverts requires time, empathy, and knowledge of their communication preferences and styles. This chapter will discuss tactics for encouraging effective and beneficial negotiations with introverts in various settings, including business and personal agreements.

Establish a relaxed and welcoming atmosphere for negotiations, giving introverts the room and time they require to voice their ideas and worries. Promote candid communication and teamwork instead of forcing people to make judgments quickly or putting them under pressure.

To illustrate, John, an introverted businessman, feels overpowered by the intense environment and quick-talking topics during contract talks. Recognizing that he is uncomfortable, his counterpart offers a break so that they may gather themselves and discuss the subject from a different angle. With this

strategy, John can better collect his thoughts and communicate his worries, resulting in a more fruitful and successful negotiation.

Show empathy and compassion for introverts' needs and priorities by actively and intently listening to their viewpoints and worries. Clarify unclear topics and pose insightful questions to ensure everyone knows each other's goals and interests.

Look for areas of agreement and investigate original ideas that consider both sides' interests and worries. Promote brainstorming and teamwork to produce creative ideas and alternatives. Having alternatives will help build a sense of cooperation and partnership during the negotiating process.

You can facilitate effective and fruitful talks with introverts by establishing a cooperative and encouraging atmosphere, actively listening to their viewpoints, and seeking innovative

solutions that consider the interests of both sides.

Questions for contemplation:

- *How can you make negotiations with introverts feel relaxed and unthreatening?*
- *What techniques can you use to hear the opinions and worries of introverts when negotiating actively?*
- *When negotiating with introverts, how can you find common ground and consider innovative ideas considering both sides' interests?*

CHAPTER 13

RESOLVING CONFLICT WITH AN INTROVERT

"Less drama, more books." – Unknown

- Be kind and sympathetic when resolving conflicts.
- Use good communication skills and active listening.
- Develop win-win solutions.

Effective communication techniques, tolerance, and empathy are necessary for resolving disputes with introverts. This chapter will discuss methods for handling disagreements in a polite, constructive way that respects the needs and preferences of introverts.

Be kind and sympathetic when resolving conflicts, considering introverts must digest their feelings and ideas before participating in conversations. Give them the room and time to consider the circumstances and find their unique way of expressing themselves.

To illustrate: A couple named Sarah and David can't agree on what to do this weekend. While David, an extrovert, wants to go out and socialize with friends, Sarah, an introvert, would rather spend a quiet weekend at home. David allows Sarah time to consider her options and voice her worries rather than forcing her to decide immediately. With this method, Sarah can calmly express her

***preferences, and they can devise a solution
that meets their wants.***

During talks about conflict resolution, use
good communication skills and active listening.
Encourage introverts to express their ideas and
worries honestly and openly by showing them
that you understand and value their viewpoints
and emotions.

Look for areas of agreement and investigate
solutions that consider all parties' needs and
desires. Together, they devise a variety of com-
promises and alternate options. The goal is to
develop win-win solutions that respect introverts' comfort levels and preferences.

You may handle disagreements with introverts
in a respectful, productive way that builds
rapport and promotes understanding by taking
an empathic, proactive listening approach to
conflict resolution and concentrating on creating creative solutions.

Questions for contemplation:

- *How do you facilitate a conversation about dispute resolution in which introverts feel comfortable expressing themselves?*
- *What techniques can you use to engage introverts in productive conversation and active listening while resolving conflicts?*
- *When resolving conflicts, how can you find common ground and investigate options that respect introverts' inclinations and comfort levels?*

CHAPTER 14

INCLUDING AN INTROVERT IN GROUP ACTIVITIES

"I am rarely bored alone; I am often bored in groups and crowds." – Laurie Helgoe

- Establish a warm, accepting environment.
- Encourage them to do so in ways that suit their preferences.

- Give them time to withdraw from the group and refuel.

Given introverts' inclinations for solitude and social engagement, incorporating them into group activities takes tact and understanding. In this chapter, we'll look at ways to make social gatherings, team projects, and community activities feel like safe spaces for introverts to feel appreciated and included.

Establish a warm, accepting environment where introverts may express themselves and take things on their own time. Instead of forcing them to participate in activities that might feel overwhelming or putting them under pressure, please encourage them to do so in ways that suit their preferences and comfort level.

To illustrate: Alex's book club meets monthly to discuss the books they've recently finished reading. Because she knows that some members are quiet and might find it challenging to speak up in conversations with large groups,

Alex includes structured activities like written reflections or small group discussions to ensure everyone can contribute and express their opinions.

Give introverts the chance to contribute in ways that suit their preferences and strengths. Give them assignments that let them work alone or in smaller groups and be sure to acknowledge and value their contributions to the team's overall success.

Schedule downtime and solitude periods to accommodate introverts' desire to get breaks and time to recharge during group activities. Give them time to withdraw from the group and refuel so they can contribute thoroughly and actively without feeling overburdened.

You can ensure that introverts feel appreciated and included in group events by fostering a friendly and inclusive environment, allowing them to participate in ways that play according

to their strengths, and honoring their need for privacy and downtime.

Questions for contemplation:

- *How can you foster a friendly, accepting environment where introverts feel free to join in activities with others at their own pace?*
- *What positions and responsibilities can you give introverts that best suit their contributions and strengths?*
- *How can you accommodate introverts' need for pauses and time to recharge during group events to ensure that they feel included and at ease?*

UNDERSTANDING AN INTROVERT'S NEED FOR ALONE TIME

"The highest form of love is to be the protector of another person's solitude." – Rainer Maria Rilke

- Introverts require time to recover and refuel.
- When introverts need solitude, give them space and privacy.

- Urge introverts to prioritize self-care.

Accommodating an introvert's desire for solitude is crucial to developing a positive and satisfying connection with them. This chapter will examine the causes of introverts' preference for isolation and strategies for appreciating and fostering this need.

Understand that introverts require time to recover and refuel following social engagements and stimuli. Unlike extroverts, who thrive on socializing, Introverts need time to digest their ideas, reflect on experiences, and replenish their psychological and emotional reserves.

To illustrate, Sarah, an introvert, feels mentally exhausted and overstimulated by the continuous social interactions after attending a busy networking event. When she gets home, she lets herself have the alone time to unwind and refuel by spending the evening reading a book in her favorite quiet corner.

Sarah will be mentally and emotionally prepared for the next day.

When introverts need solitude, give them space and privacy to honor their boundaries and preferences. When they withdraw, don't take it personally or pressure them to interact with others; instead, be patient and supportive of their need for personal time to recover.

Urge introverts to prioritize self-care and make time for soul-nourishing and energy-replenishing activities. Activities that enable introverts to connect with themselves and discover inner peace are beneficial to them. These activities include reading a book, solo walking outdoors, and practicing meditation.

Acknowledging and respecting introverts' need for alone time can improve your relationship and foster a friendly atmosphere where they feel appreciated and understood.

Questions for contemplation:

- *How do you read and honor an introvert's cues that they need time alone?*
- *What tactics can you use to help and motivate introverts to value their alone time and self-care?*
- *How do you create a mutually respectful and understanding relationship while respecting introverted people who need alone time?*

CHAPTER 16

PROVIDING SPACE TO LOVE AN INTROVERT

"Kindly remove yourself from my personal space. Thanks." – Gemma Correll

- Providing an introvert with space shows affection.
- Know that their need for privacy doesn't indicate how they feel about you.

- Talk openly about expectations and boundaries.

Understanding and honoring an introvert's demand for privacy and independence in a relationship is a necessary part of loving them. This chapter will discuss respecting an introvert's desire for privacy and personal space while fostering a happy and healthy relationship.

Acknowledge that providing an introvert with space shows affection and regard for their uniqueness and independence. Recognize that introverts require time alone to refuel and find calm and that giving them the necessary space is essential to promoting their happiness and general well-being.

Allowing introverts to withdraw and refuel without interference or pressure shows respect for their personal limits and alone-time preferences. Recognize that their need for privacy does not indicate how they feel about

you, so try not to take it personally when they ask for space and fight the urge to get closer to them continuously.

To illustrate, John understands that his introverted partner appreciates solitude and personal space in their relationship. John gives his partner space to relax and refuel when they indicate a need for alone time by not starting pointless discussions or activities.

Promote candid dialogue and understanding about each other's requirements for privacy and alone time in the partnership. Talk openly about expectations and boundaries and collaborate to strike a balance that honors each partner's needs for autonomy and connection.

To illustrate, Long-term partners Sarah and David freely discuss their privacy and space requirements. They ensure each partner feels appreciated and understood by setting clear expectations and boundaries around alone time. Over time, they grow and strengthen

their connection by encouraging open communication and understanding.

You may build a caring and encouraging relationship that respects an introvert's uniqueness and deepens your bond as a pair by acknowledging and accepting their need for solitude.

Questions for contemplation:

- *How can you appreciate and show love for an introvert by understanding that they require time alone and space in the relationship?*
- *What techniques can you use to honor an introvert's privacy and solitude desires?*
- *How can you help the couple respect each other's desire for privacy and alone time by encouraging honest dialogue and understanding?*

CHAPTER 17

COPING WITH INTROVERTS

"Friends are those rare people who ask how we are, and then wait to hear the answer." –
Ed Cunningham

- Accept that people have different personalities.
- Engage in active listening.
- Avoid overstimulating introverts with excessive socializing.

Understanding an introvert's wants and preferences and creating a harmonic, supportive relationship is vital to coping with them.
This chapter will discuss how to deal with introverts in various contexts, including friendships, professional situations, and personal relationships.

Acknowledge and respect the distinctions between introverts and extroverts, considering that the former may have distinct energy levels, social preferences, and communication styles. Accept that people have different personalities, and when you interact with introverts, keep an open mind and be prepared to adjust to meet their requirements.

Modify your expectations and communication style to suit introverts' tastes and comfort levels better. Engage in active listening, pose open-ended questions, and give introverts space to express themselves at their own pace

to build rapport and a deeper understanding in your exchanges.

To illustrate: Tanya is an introvert, while Tony, an extrovert, is close to her. Tanya appreciates more private activities and deep chats with one person, while Tony enjoys regular socializing and impromptu outings. They strike a balance that lets them enjoy each other's company while respecting their individuality despite their disparities in tastes.

Avoid overstimulating introverts with excessive socializing or attention-seeking and respect their boundaries and desires for alone time. Recognize that their desire for solitude is crucial to their happiness and well-being and provide them with the room and flexibility to refuel on their own.

You may build gratifying and encouraging relationships with introverts who recognize their uniqueness and promote mutual

understanding and progress by treating them with sensitivity, adaptability, and respect.

To illustrate: Emily, a manager, oversees a group of both extroverted and introverted people. To ensure that every voice is heard and respected, she allows introverts to share their ideas and opinions during team meetings without interjecting. By adapting her communication approach to suit the requirements of introverts, Emily cultivates a cooperative and welcoming team environment.

Questions for contemplation:

- *How can you modify your expectations and communication style to better suit introverts' comfort levels and preferences?*
- *What techniques can you use in your interactions to honor introverts' boundaries and need for alone time?*

- *How can you develop empathy and understanding to create a harmonic and supporting dynamic in your connections with introverts?*

CONCLUSION

Comprehending and engaging with introverts requires empathy, tolerance, and reciprocal regard. This book covers a lot of ground about introversion and offers doable tactics for building deep bonds, encouraging personal development, and creating happy relationships with introverts.

The most important thing to remember is that introverts thrive when their distinct traits and preferences are acknowledged, recognized, and supported, and this includes understanding how to communicate effectively, establish inclusive environments, and respect introverts' desire for privacy and independence.

By valuing empathy and sensitivity, we can create environments where introverts feel heard, seen, and valued for who they are. The

ways we can better understand and engage with introverts in business, social situations, and personal relationships are universal, strengthening our bonds and improving our well-being as a group.

Remember to approach every interaction with introverts with interest, understanding, and an open heart as you continue to know and engage with them. Doing so will build stronger bonds with introverts and make the world more accepting and compassionate.

ABOUT THE AUTHOR

Antonia O. Allen was born in Jamaica, West Indies, and lives in New York, where she navigates both the corporate and entrepreneurial worlds.

Antonia was inspired to advocate for the introverted community because of her experiences of being misunderstood and undervalued in her personal and professional surroundings. Her experiences of being called "weird" and feeling invisible in social settings inspired her to write her first book, ***Unlocking the Introvert: A Pocket Guide to Understanding and Interacting with Introverts***. Through this book, Antonia hopes to highlight the complex inner lives of introverts and promote their acceptance in a society where they frequently feel disregarded.

Antonia's mission is to bridge the communication gap between extroverts and introverts by fostering empathy and understanding.

Her deep understanding of introverts' unique needs and strengths serves to strengthen relationships in personal and professional settings. Through her book, Antonia aspires to empower introverts to embrace their unique strengths and enlighten extroverts about the nuances of introverted behavior. She hopes her readers will discover the tools to build stronger, more empathetic connections across the spectrum of personality types, and supporting and enriching their lives.

Made in the USA
Columbia, SC
03 September 2024

41645683R00052